What's Inside Is Inside Me, Too

My Chromosomes Make Me Unique

Written by Deslie Quinby and
Jeannie Visootsak, MD
Illustrated by Michael Johnson

ISBN-13: 978-0692310380
ISBN-10: 069231038X

2

About the Authors

DESLIE QUINBY was welcomed into the world of Down syndrome when her son JC was born with Down syndrome in 2004. Since then she has been an advocate and champion for her son and active in the Atlanta Down syndrome community. Deslie has her first Master's degree from the George Washington University and her second Master's from the Sloan School of Management at MIT. She is an accomplished businesswoman, having held executive positions at ChoicePoint, Carlson Wagonlit Travel, and The Weather Channel. She has also had experience running her own businesses. She is the mother of two boys: JC, age 10, and Skyler, age 9.

JEANNIE VISOOTSAK, MD, FAAP, ASSOCIATE PROFESSOR, is a board-certified Developmental-Behavioral Pediatrician at Emory University School of Medicine, Atlanta, GA. She is also the Medical Director of the Down Syndrome Clinic and Down Syndrome Clinical Trial Unit at Emory University. The Down Syndrome Clinic was established in 2003 to meet the needs of families and children with Down syndrome. Dr. Visootsak also serves on the Professional Advisory Council for the National Down Syndrome Congress and is an Advisory Board Member on the Down Syndrome Association of Atlanta.

MICHAEL JOHNSON is an illustrator and graphic artist living in Atlanta, GA. He is currently an undergraduate student at Georgia State University. He previously studied at the Art Institute of Atlanta in their Game Art and Design program. He has illustrated several children's books related to genetic conditions, including Joe Learns About Fabry Disease, My Brother, MPS, and Me!, and Super Pompe.

3

Little chromosome pairs
Make up lions, penguins and hares.

In fact, they make up all living things,
Even teachers and mommies and kings.

5

These chromosomes, they provide direction,
Shaping and molding, creating perfection.

6

Yes, they are really powerful things.
Helping create life and all living beings.

Providing blueprints for humans and animals, too,
Making dogs bark, cats meow, roosters crow and cows moo.

8

So how many chromosomes are inside you and me?
Forty-six, as you will see.

Twenty-three pairs, half from mom, half from dad,
Making forty-six total for you lasses and lads.

They decide the color of your eyes, your hair and your skin.
They can make you real big, real strong or real thin.

11

Think of them as tiny maps.

Always working. They get no naps.

You ask, what would happen if you had just one more?
Would that be possible? What would be in store?

13

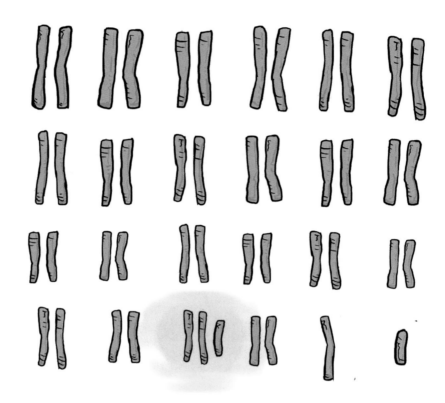

Forty-seven chromosomes? It does happen some.
It's called Down syndrome, trisomy 21.

Folks with Down syndrome, they exist everywhere.
It's unique, this is true, but it's not really that rare.

In fact, you may know someone with trisomy 21.
If you do, then you know they can be lots of fun.

16

They love to dance, to sing and to play.

They are unique (like you are). They do things their way.

17

They laugh. They cry. They smile. They pout.
You'll always know they love you, without the slightest doubt.

18

Our chromosomes, they provide individual flair.
So, love your differences like your lungs love the air.

19

Because, no matter the number, no matter the day,
You and your chromosomes are here to stay.

Say thanks to your chromosomes for all that they do,
Because they are the things that make you, you.

21

So now that you know about chromosome pairs.
How they make you unique, special and rare,

22

Please, remember that, black or white, big or small,
We need each other – differences and all.

Down Syndrome 101

WHERE DID THE NAME DOWN SYNDROME COME FROM?

In 1866, Dr. John Langdon Down described a group of patients who looked and acted very much alike, despite no familial relation. It was a puzzle to him: Why did these patients have so much in common? He revealed that they had language problems and simultaneously exhibited sociability and humor. "Down syndrome" was coined to recognize Dr. John Langdon Down's immense contribution to the diagnosis. His investigations have since helped countless children and families, as Down syndrome turns out to be quite common. In fact, according to current statistics, it is present in approximately 1 in every 691 births, approximately 6000 births per year in the US. It is present in all ethnic groups, socioeconomic levels, and geographic regions.

WHAT ARE THE CHARACTERISTICS OF DOWN SYNDROME?

Doctors often diagnose a baby with Down syndrome shortly after birth because they observe characteristic physical features and low muscle tone (hypotonia). Facial features characteristic of Down syndrome can be quite variable, but often include upslanting eyes, epicanthal folds (small folds of skin at the inside corners of the eyes), a small nose, a tongue that may protrude, and small ears. Some babies will have an extra fold of skin on the back of their neck and a single transverse crease across one or both palms. Every child is different, so you may not see all or any of these features.

WHAT IS THE CAUSE OF DOWN SYNDROME?

A blood test is done to confirm the diagnosis of Down syndrome. It is sent to a genetic laboratory for chromosome studies. Chromosomes carry genes that determine our make-up.

24

The typical number of human chromosomes is 46 and they come in pairs numbered 1 through 22, in addition to the sex chromosomes, XX for girls and XY for boys. Chromosomal karyotype for Down syndrome will typically show three copies of chromosome 21 (95% of Down syndrome cases have this type, known as standard trisomy 21). But there are three different types of Down syndrome: standard trisomy 21, mosaicism, and translocation. Mosaicism is the rarest version of Down syndrome. A child with mosaicism has some cells with the third copy of chromosome 21 and other cells without the extra copy. The ratio of trisomy cells to non-trisomy cells can vary. In translocation, a portion of chromosome 21 breaks off and attaches to another chromosome. This results in a child having three copies of the information from chromosome 21.

HOW WILL MY CHILD LEARN AND DEVELOP?

Children with Down syndrome will learn like any other child. By tracking a child's developmental milestones, parents, physicians, and therapists are able to monitor a child's learning, behavior, and development, and mark the child's progress along his/her developmental journey. The term milestones is derived from the word "stone marker", which is placed along the road to indicate distance traveled. To develop is to expand or realize the potentialities of; bring to fuller, greater, or better state.

Development is commonly discussed in terms of domains of function. Gross motor skills refer to the use of large muscles of the body; fine motor skills refer to the use of small muscles of the hands; language refers to the comprehension (receptive language) and production (expressive language) of meaningful symbolic communication; and social functioning refers to emotional reactions to events and interactions with others. The range of developmental milestones in children with Down syndrome is wide, and may be impacted by medical issues (e.g., seizures, hearing loss). It is important for parents to know what is within the expected range, and to make sure that their child is progressing appropriately.

25

How can I maximize my child's potential?

Your child will be referred to the state's Early Intervention Program shortly after birth to ensure that he continues to make progress with the long-term goal of maximizing his potential. Early Intervention is a plan of active commitment to the wellbeing of infants and toddlers with special needs that focuses on gathering beneficial interventional resources as soon as possible. Adopting an early-intervention mindset is key to ensuring that your baby develops as successfully as possible.

The diagnosis of Down syndrome most certainly does not imply a lack of development. A child with Down syndrome is expected to progress functionally in all areas of development, including gross motor, fine motor, language, and social. The rate at which your baby acquires some of these skills may vary, but your child will continue to make progress. In any case, remember that your child will follow a positive trajectory when it comes to these milestones, if you first believe that he or she can, and second, if you choose to work closely with the guidance of interventional therapists. It will be of great reassurance and relief for you to know that, as part of the Early Intervention plan, there is a wealth of community support in the form therapies from birth to age 3 (physical, occupational, and speech, among others) for babies with Down syndrome. These therapies will continue when the child starts school. Furthermore, additional resources and support will be recommended to ensure that your child is making progress academically.

Be your child's advocate! Talk to your child's therapists and teachers. Share information about your child's strengths and challenges with them. Collaborate with them in designing a plan of action that will help your child's reach his full potential. With appropriate and ongoing interventional therapies and resources, your child will make progress. Your child will be able to do many things. He will be able read, write, sing, dance, swim, run, etc... He will love you and make you smile and laugh.

And don't forget to take a break and enjoy yourself! Being a parent is a lot of work and can be stressful at times.

26

WHAT ARE THE HEALTH PROBLEMS ASSOCIATED WITH DOWN SYNDROME?

The Down Syndrome Medical Interest Group and the Committee on Genetics of the American Academy of Pediatrics have developed health supervision guidelines for managing the care of children with Down syndrome. There are several health issues that occur occasionally in children with Down syndrome. Below is a list of some medical issues commonly seen in children with Down syndrome.

- Approximately 50% of newborns with Down syndrome will have a congenital heart defect. An evaluation by a pediatric cardiologist, including an echocardiogram, is recommended in all newborns with Down syndrome.

-Hearing evaluations is done at birth, 6 months, at 12 months, and once a year thereafter. Referral to a pediatric otolaryngologist (ears, nose, and throat doctor) is recommended if the eardrum is not visualized and/or ear infections occur frequently.

-Thyroid studies are done at birth. If the newborn screen is normal, a follow-up for thyroid function test is recommended at 6 months and then yearly.

-Children with Down syndrome should have an eye evaluation by a pediatric ophthalmologist within the first 6 months of age and yearly thereafter until age 5. If no vision problems exist, ophthalmology exams can take place every 2 years from ages 5 to 13 and every 3 years from ages 13 to 21.

Other issues may include gastrointestinal and respiratory problems, sleep apnea, dry skin, obesity, and constipation. It is important for your child to be monitored closely by his pediatrician and/or specialists. You should also ask questions and discuss your concerns with your child's physician. When your child is healthy, he will be able to function and learn better.

27

Made in United States
North Haven, CT
23 February 2022

Every child, every person, every living thing is unique, in big part, due to chromosomes. Children with Down syndrome have an extra chromosome. This book aims to inform people about Down syndrome in a full illustrative way. In the process, it also explains chromosomes and their role in making every living thing special. This book serves as a valuable tool for educators, siblings, individuals with Down syndrome, advocates, and for those innately curious.

$7.9
ISBN 978-0-692-31038-
5079

9 780692 310380